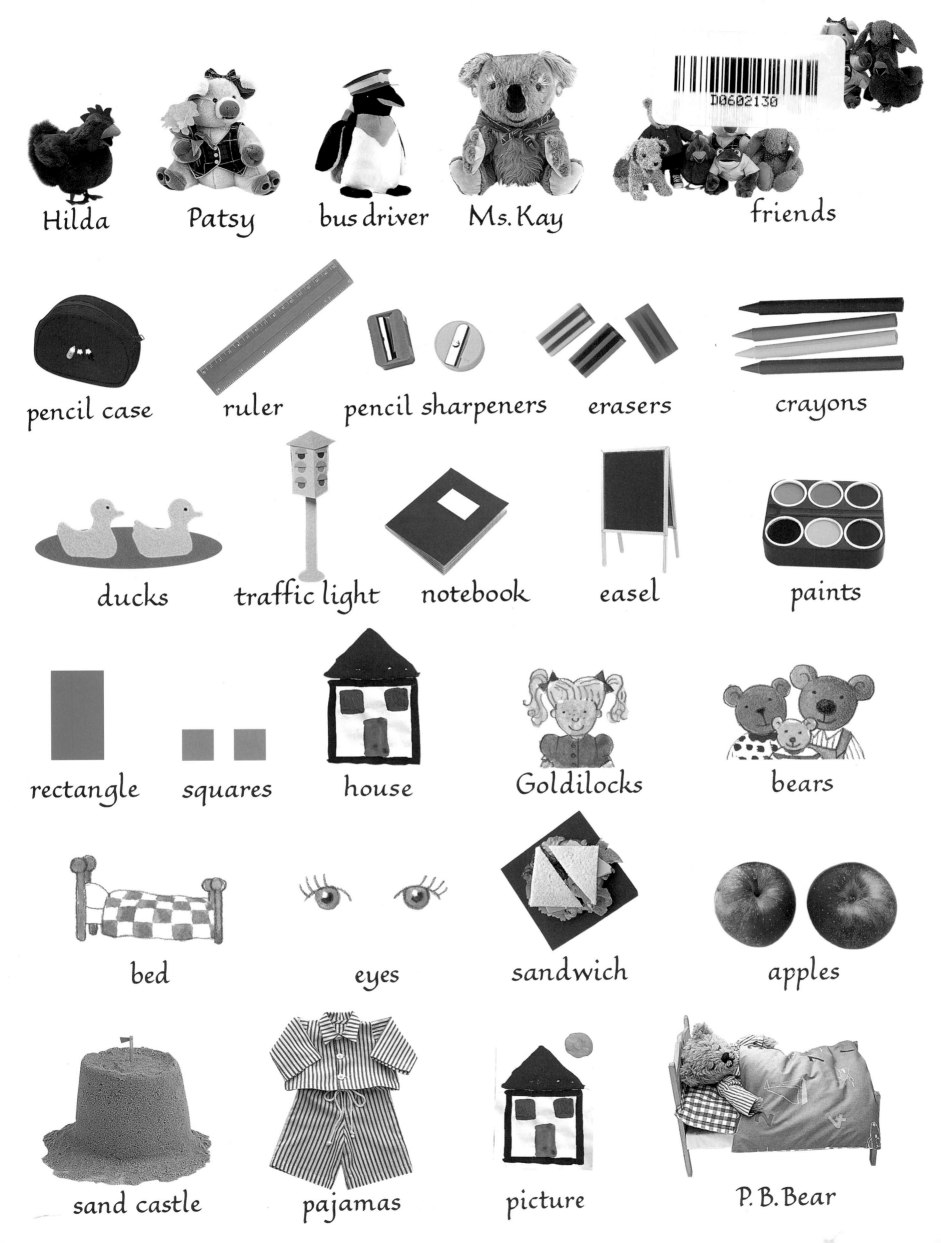

Hilda

Patsy

bus driver

Ms. Kay

friends

pencil case

ruler

pencil sharpeners

erasers

crayons

ducks

traffic light

notebook

easel

paints

rectangle

squares

house

Goldilocks

bears

bed

eyes

sandwich

apples

sand castle

pajamas

picture

P. B. Bear

A DK PUBLISHING BOOK

Managing Art Editor Chris Fraser
Art Editor Claire Jones
Project Editor Caryn Jenner
Production Louise Barratt
Photography Dave King

First American Edition, 1996
2 4 6 8 10 9 7 5 3

Published in the United States
by DK Publishing, Inc.,
95 Madison Avenue, New York, New York 10016
Visit us on the World Wide Web at
http://www.dk.com

A CIP catalog record is available
from the Library of Congress.

ISBN 0-7894-1172-5

Colour reproduction by Colourscan, Singapore
Printed and bound in Italy by L.E.G.O.

Acknowledgments
DK would like to thank the following manufacturers
for permission to photograph copyright material:
Ty Inc. for "Toffee" the dog and "Freddie" the frog
The Manhattan Toy Company Ltd. for "Antique Rabbit"
Folkmanis Inc. for "Furry Folk" hen puppet
D.S. Nicholass Limited for the toy pig
Althans KG. for the Althans Club koala bear and penguin

DK would also like to thank the following people
for their help in producing this book:
Barbara Owen, Robert Fraser, Stephen Raw, Fiona Munro,
Natascha Biebow, Vera Jones, Alice and Edward Nash

Can you find the little bear
in each scene?

P.B. BEAR'S SCHOOL DAY

Lee Davis

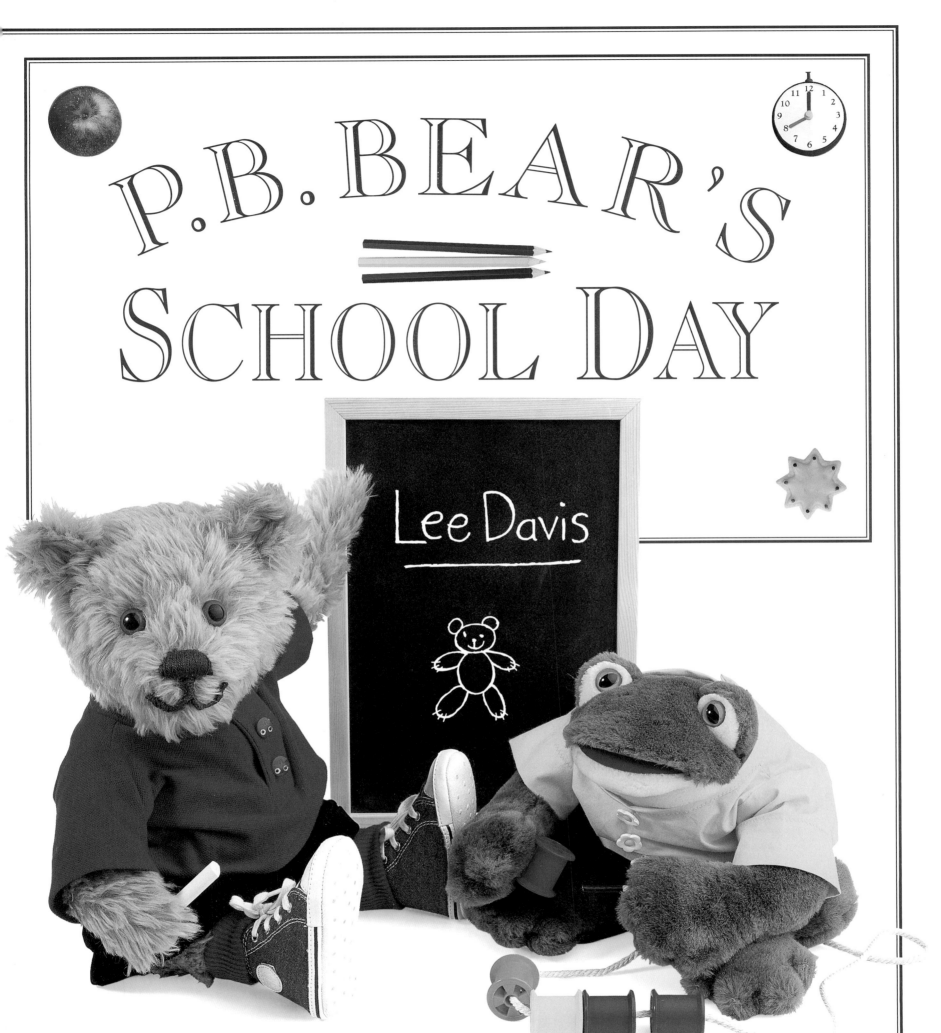

DK

Brrring! went the  . Wake up!

Quickly, P.B. Bear jumped out of and

put on his and . Then he found his

and his . In his , he put 1 , 2 ,

3 , 4 , and 5 . Then he

put his into his and ran out the .

Oh dear! hurried back. He'd almost forgotten

his .

Now he was ready for school!

and his friend Dermott rode the

they called to the as they drove past. At the next **BUS STOP**, Hilda and Patsy

shouted, "Go!" "Here we are," said the

when they arrived at school.

Can you count how many of us ride on the bus?

 and his  went into the school.

Ms. Kay , the teacher, said good morning.

"Good morning!" called . He liked .

 took his and a ✏ from

his . He wrote his name very carefully

in the [ ] : P and B for P.B. Bear.

What else begins with a P or a B?

What things begin with the first letter

of your name?

set up an [easel] and [paints] .

put on his painting [smock] and found his [paintbrush] .

He shared the  with  and  and  . What a mess!

First  painted a  . Then he painted a  with a  on top . Inside the  , he painted

1  and 2 little  . It was a  !

What color  did  use?

"It's story time," said .

She began to read the story of and the 3  .

All of the  joined in at their favorite part.

When the 3 arrived home,

Father said, "Who's been sitting in my ?"

Mother  said, "Who's been eating my ?"

Baby said, "Who is sleeping in my bed ?"

All 3 bears looked in the bed .

Goldilocks opened her eyes .

"Oh dear!" she said.

At lunchtime,  sat outside with his . He opened his .

It was packed full! ate his ,

then took 2 from his .

He gave 1 to .

How many apples did have left?

2-1=1

had 2 🍪🍪 in his 🧰 .

Then 🐸 gave him 2 more 💗🔷 .

How many cookies did 🐕 have then?

$$2+2=4$$

🧸 had eaten his 🥪 , his 🍎 ,

his 🍰 , and his 🥄 .

Now his 🧰 was empty!

After lunch,  and his played until the came to take them home again.

Who is at the top?

Who is down?

Who is at the bottom?

Whose  is big?

Whose is little?

Who is up?

Soon it was time to go home.

Good-bye, . See you tomorrow!

That night,  was very sleepy. He'd had a busy day

at school! He took his  out of his  .

Then he put on his  and climbed into  .

Soon he was smiling in his sleep.

Sweet dreams,  !

P. B. Bear Dermott Russell Franny

alarm clock bed pants shirt schoolbag

pencils door lunch box bus

bus stop

smock paintbrush circle square triangle

Father Bear Mother Bear Baby Bear chair porridge

cookies lunch box cake yogurt